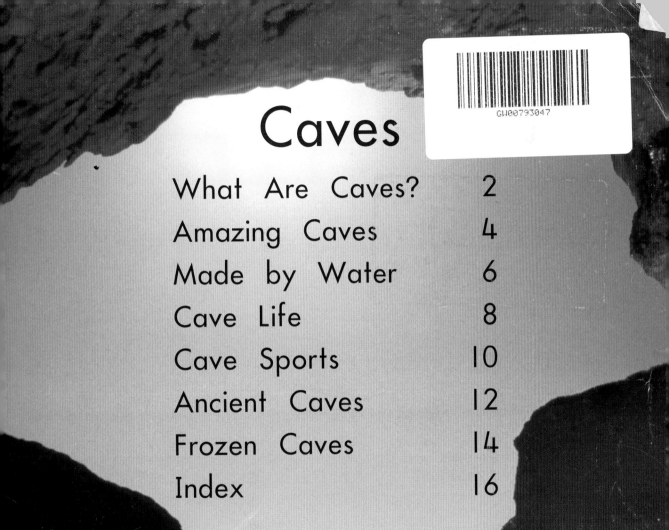

Caves

What Are Caves?

A cave is a hollow space in the earth. Some caves are near the sea. Others are in mountains, deserts, or forests. Some caves are deep under the ground.

3

Amazing Caves

Some caves have amazing features, such as strange rock shapes. Some of these caves are famous.

Rock shapes like these that point down are *stalactites*. Those that point up are *stalagmites*.

The longest cave system in the world is the Mammoth-Flint Ridge Cave System, in Kentucky, U.S.A.

Made by Water

Many caves are made by water wearing away rock. This takes a very long time.

Moving water can wear away rock, leaving a hard rock cave.

Cave Life

Caves provide homes for many animals. Some insects, spiders, lizards, birds, and bats live in caves.

Cave spider

Glow-worm

Many bats like the cool,
dark dampness of caves.

Cave Sports

For some people, exploring caves can be a hobby or sport. These *cavers* sometimes go into dark and dangerous places, so they need special clothes and equipment.

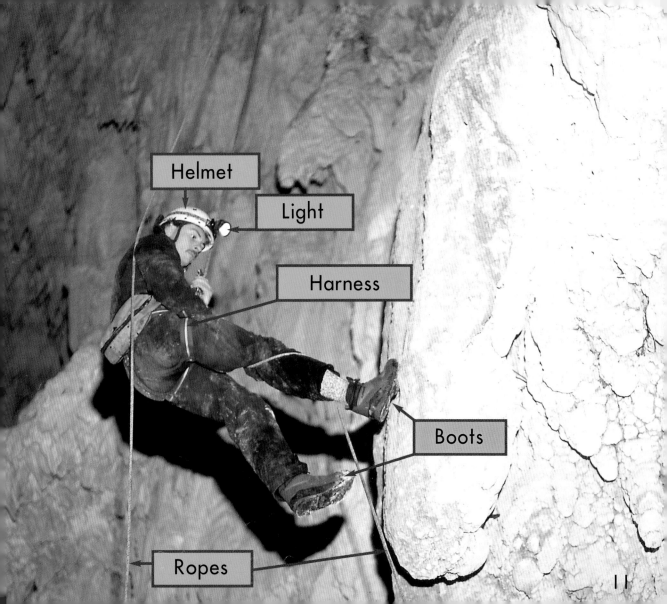

Helmet

Light

Harness

Boots

Ropes

11

Ancient Caves

Some caves have ancient paintings on their walls. These paintings can help us learn about people who lived thousands of years ago.

Many cave paintings show animals that were hunted for food.

Frozen Caves

Most caves are made of rock, but some are made of ice and snow.

Ice cave

Cavers who explore
ice caves use
ice axes and wear
boots with spikes.

Index